EVERYTHIN_ ___ _
EVER WANTED TO
KNOW ABOUT
TOMATOES & SEX
BUT WERE
AFRAID TO ASK

**A Prize Collection of
Tomato Trivia, Jokes,
Remedies, Superstitions, Beauty
Aids, Household Hints, Sex
&
Treasured Fried Green
Tomato Recipes**

$10.00

Gift copies of this book can be ordered at
www.robertwpelton.com
or
amazon.com
or
createspace.com/5180839

Printed in America
On Recycled Paper
In
Charleston, South Carolina

&

Published in America
By
Tomato Press International
Knoxville, Tennessee

Try to Always Buy American
Made Products

4

Copyright © 2015
By
Robert W. Pelton

Tomato Press International

First Edition

5

CONTENTS

PART I
TOMATO TRIVIA

PART II
BEAUTY TIPS,
HOME REMEDIES
&
HOUSEHOLD HINTS

PART III
APHROSDIASIC
QUALITIES
OF TOMATOES!

PART IV
A TOUCH OF TOMATO
HUMOR

PART V
TOMATOES & BETTER
HEALTH?

PART VI
MORE UNIQUE TOMATO
RECIPES

PART VII

PART 1

TOMATO
TRIVIA

1

Everything You Ever Wanted To Know About Tomatoes But Were Afraid to Ask!

The tomato a fruit or vegetable?

It's a fruit by definition.

The *Webster School & Office Dictionary* defines a tomato as *"The pulpy, edible fruit of a plant."*

It's defined by *The American Heritage Dictionary* in this manner: *"A fleshy, smooth-skinned reddish fruit, eaten as a vegetable."*

The tomato is both the official state fruit and the official state vegetable in Arkansas.

And tomato juice is Ohio's official state beverage.

How many different varieties of tomatoes are there?

The U.S. Department of Agriculture reports that there are 25,000 varieties of tomatoes.

And that's a fact!

The heaviest recorded tomato ever grown was in Edmond, Oklahoma, in 1986.

It weighed an incredible seven pounds 12 ounces!

The Aztecs ate tomatoes?

They certainly did!

Tomatoes were cultured by these ancient people as early as 700 AD.

The Incas are believed to have also cultured tomatoes during this same period of time.

Tomatoes were thought to have originated in Peru.

Their name comes from the Aztec *"xitomati"*.

Translated this means *"plump thing with a navel"*.

Some researchers say the name is derived from *"tomati,"* its name in *"Nahuati,"* the Aztec language.

When the tomato was introduced to Europe in the 1500s Germans called the fruit *"the apple of paradise."*

The French called the tomato *"The seed of love."*

Tomatoes in Germany are called *"lycopersicon lycopersicum"* which translates to *"wolf peach."*

Germans avoided eating tomatoes in the 1700s as they considered them to be poisonous.

Although tomatoes are perfectly safe and healthy to eat, the leaves of the plant are known to be toxic (poisonous).

Witches in Germany are said to have used tomato plants filled with unripe green tomatoes to summon or bring forth werewolves.

Tomatoes in 17th Century England were called tomatos.

This was later changed to tomato due to the more familiar potato.

Here's what a tomato is called in other languages:

Danish -- *tomet*

Dutch -- *tomaat*

French -- *tomate*

German – *Tomate*

Italian -- *pomodoro*

Spanish -- *tomate*

Most tomatoes grown in 17th Century England were yellow.

Yellow tomatoes at this time were considered to be poisonous.

However, red and green tomatoes were regularly eaten.

Yellow tomatoes were then commonly used for decorating and placed around the house because of their beauty.

Around 1690 tomato ketchup was first mentioned in print.

Ketchup as a word was derived from China's Ke-tsiap which was a pickled fish sauce.

Joe Campbell developed the idea of condensing tomato soup in 1897.

He did this for a practical reason.

By decreasing the water content in soup, shipping costs were reduced as was the amount of storage space required.

Tomato juice was first blended with the juices of other vegetables in 1948.

The tasty combination was sold by the Campbell Soup Company as V-8 Juice.

Ronald Reagan, later to become President of the United States, was one of Campbell Soup Company's first spokesmen for their V-8 advertisements.

Now 65% of chefs throughout the world reportedly use canned tomatoes in their recipes.

Why?

For convenience.

The consistent quality.

Flavor that is consistently the same.

Tomato consumption in America has increased more than 30% over the last two decades.

The Increase is mostly in prepared forms such as tomato paste, salsa, spaghetti sauce, ketchup, etc.

One famous person who really liked ketchup was President Richard Milhous Nixon.

He often enjoyed a late night snack of cottage cheese covered with tomato ketchup.

Although a questionable conclusion, some researchers claim that Americans tend to eat more salsa than they do ketchup!

Americans consume three fourths of their tomatoes in processed form – salsa, ketchup, tomato paste, etc.

Americans eat between 22 to 24 pounds of tomatoes per person each year!

Tomatoes are America's fourth most popular fresh-market vegetable (fruit actually).

Interestingly, first, second and third most popular are potatoes, lettuce and onions.

93% of gardening households in America grow tomatoes.

Fresh-market tomatoes are grown in all 50 states.

California produces 96% of the tomatoes processed in the United States.

The world's largest tomato producer is China.

This is followed by the United States, Turkey, India and Egypt.

The tomato has a number of plant relatives.

Among tomato cousins are found the bell pepper, eggplant, potato and the extremely toxic (poisonous) belladonna which is also known as the nightshade.

Interestingly enough, nightshade has historically been used as both a poison and a medicine.

The world's biggest tomato tree?

Walt Disney's World Resort experimental greenhouse has the winner!

The tree weighs slightly more than 1,151pounds.

It yields an incredible harvest of 32,000 golf ball size tomatoes which are served at Disney World's restaurants.

At least 19 states hold annual tomato festivals.

TomatoFest in Carmel, California, features tastings of approximately 350 heirloom tomato varieties.

La Tomatina held in Valencia, Spain, is known as the messiest tomato festival in the world.

Their claim to fame is the annual tomato fight where more than 30,000 participants throw an estimated 150,000 pounds (100 metric tons) of overripe tomatoes at each other.

And lastly: Why did the odd ball artist Andy Warhol paint more than 100 pop-art works featuring Campbell tomato soup cans?

According to one widely circulated story it was simply an end result of the fact that Andy's mother had made him eat tomato soup for lunch for around 20 years!

PART 11

BEAUTY TIPS, HOME REMEDIES & HOUSEHOLD HINTS

2

Beauty Pointers
For
Women
Using Tomatoes

Tomatoes make an excellent skin treatment for everything from large pores and acne to rashes and more!

Tomatoes contain an immense amount of vitamin C and A to brighten dull skin and restore its health!

Tomatoes have cooling elements to soothe raw skin and astringents to remove excess oil!

Try the following homemade dry skin remedies using tomatoes.

You're certain to quickly see a big difference in your facial and other skin.

Opening Your Facial Pores

Slice a tomato in half.

Rub this over your face in a firm scrubbing fashion.

The high vitamin C found in the tomato will reportedly unblock your pores.

This will leave your skin feeling nicely soft and refreshed.

Getting Rid of Dry Skin

Cut a ripe tomato in 1/4 " slices.

Lay slices over your entire face.

Leave in place for 30 minutes to an hour.

The juice will loosen the top layer of your skin.

The dead skin will easily wash off after removing the tomato slices.

Make a Quick and Easy Tomato Facial

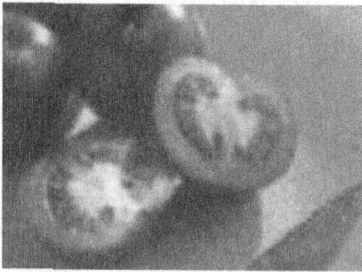

Cut a ripe tomato in half.

Gently rub the cut surface all over your face.

Press it into any visible blackheads.

Rinse and moisturize the facial skin.

That's all there is to it!

Cleansing Mask for Oily Skin

1 ripe red or yellow tomato

1 ripe avocado

A tomato-avocado facial mask is said to be great for all skin problems (oily, normal and dry).

The mixture contains the astringent, blackhead and oil reducing benefits of tomatoes with the antiseptic and moisturizing properties of avocados.

This super-rich mask also contains vitamin A, C and E.

All of these vitamins are essential for healthy skin.

To make this soothing face mask simply mash together the tomato and avocado in a small mixing bowl.

Blend well.

Smooth this paste over your face.

Leave on for a period of 20 to 30 minutes.

Then rinse off with lukewarm water.

Acne Cure Using Tomato Pulp

Mash a ripe tomato to a pulp.

Liberally apply the pulp over your facial skin.

Leave on skin for one hour.

Rinse.

Then moisturize.

Repeat this every day for several days and your acne will disappear.

To Shrink Face Pores
>1 tbls tomato juice
>4 drops lime juice

Combine the tomato juice and lime juice in a cup and blend thoroughly.

Apply this mixture to your face with a cotton ball.

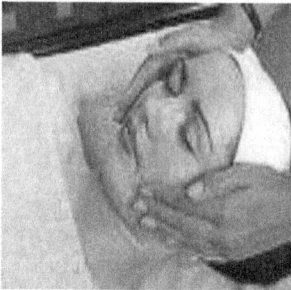

Gently massage into your skin using circular motions.

Leave on your face for 15 minutes.

Then rinse off with cool water to shrink your pores even further.

Then moisturize.

Here's a Marvelous Astringent!

To remove excess oil from your skin, simply crush a fresh ripe or yellow tomato.

Strain through a piece of cheesecloth or an old t-shirt.

Set the juice aside.

Next add a peeled and mashed cucumber to the tomato juice.

Blend well.

Apply to the skin every day with a cotton ball to keep oil and acne under control.

Tomato-Yogurt Facial Mask

Try this one if your skin is raw, irritated, itchy, blotchy, sunburned or scaly.

You'll no doubt enjoy the innumerable benefits of this wonderful yogurt and tomato mask.

Yogurt gives skin a protein boost and leaves the skin soft.

Tomato cools and neutralizes the skin's surface.

Here's how it's done:

Crush half a ripe tomato in a cup.

Add 2 tbls of plain unsweetened yogurt.

Blend thoroughly.

Spread this mixture on your face.

Leave for 20 minutes.

Then rinse off with cool water.

Get a Smooth and Glowing Face

½ cup tomato juice

1 tbls warm honey

Blend the tomato juice and honey in a small cup.

Apply to your face and neck.

Allow to remain on your skin for 15 minutes.

Rinse thoroughly.

Your skin will be smooth and glowing.

3

Old Time Tomato Remedies That Work!

Sunburn Relief

    4 tbls buttermilk

    2 tsp fresh tomato juice

Blend the buttermilk and tomato juice in a small mixing bowl or cup.

    Using a small sponge, cotton ball or your fingers, apply this mixture lightly over the sunburned areas of the skin – face, neck, arms, legs, etc.

    Leave on sunburned areas for 30 minutes.

    Very gently rinse off with cool water, Allow to dry naturally.

    Don't try to dry off with a towel!

Help With a Bad Cough

    Gargle with a shot of freshly squeezed tomato juice.

    The effect is said to be quick and miraculous!

Gargling for a Sore Throat

Take a tablespoon of freshly squeezed tomato juice.

Blend with a teaspoon of freshly squeezed lemon juice.

Gargle for 12 seconds.

Then swallow the mixture,

This wills sooth a sore throat.

To Help a Sickly Person

According to tradition, put an overripe tomato under the bed of a sick person.

He or she should be cured by the time the tomato begins to rot.

Slugs In Your Tomato Patch?

Make a beer trap!

It's easy and quick.

And it catches and kills slugs!

Simply take an ordinary Ball pint canning jar.

Dig a suitable hole in the dirt.

Set the canning jar in this hole.

Pat the dirt around it.

The mouth or opening must be level with the soil.

Then fill the jar with beer until it is 1/4" from the top of the jar,

Slugs are attracted to the smell of the beer.

Therefore they'll crawl into the canning jar and get stuck in the beer.

End of problem!

Growing Tomatoes In the Country?

You might have a problem with deer sneaking in and devouring your tomatoes.

What can you do?

It's simple and inexpensive!

Put four fresh eggs and a quart of water in your blender.

When thoroughly blended pour the mixture into a spray bottle.

Spray your tomato plants with a little of this mixture.

The deer will leave them alone because they can't stand the smell of eggs.

Keeping Insects Off the Leaves

1 cup hot peppers   2 cups water
Put the ingredients in a blender.
Pulverize!
Strain if needed.

Put this mixture in a spray bottle.

Spray on your tomato plants.

Bugs don't like the smell of pepper and will leave your tomato plants alone.

Repelling Insects

Blend one gallon of water and 2 tbls liquid soap.

Fill a spray bottle with this mixture.

Lightly spray your tomato plants.

The soap dissolves the wax layer on the leaves.

This causes insects to dry out and die.

Sure Cure For a Headache

Put a wooden match in your hair while weeding a tomato patch.

This simple remedy is said by some to be a good way of getting rid of a persistent headache.

Problem With a Nosebleed?
Attach a small piece of lead to a string.

A lead fishing sinker will do the job.

Wear this around your neck.

Slowly walk between the rows of tomato plants in a tomato patch.

This should stop your nose bleed!

Tired and Aching Feet?
Take off your shoes and socks.

Walk barefoot all around in your tomato garden.

This will put an end to tired and aching feet.

Problem With Cramping?

Wear a rubber band on your wrist while weeding your tomato bed.

This simple act is said to prevent leg cramps as well as any other kind.

How About Rheumatism?

Wrap a simple piece of copper wire around your left ankle.

Work in your tomato patch while wearing the copper ankle bracelet.

This is believed by some to be a reliable cure for rheumatism.

Arthritis Cure?

Here's a simple but reportedly effective cure for arthritis.

Just carry a shriveled potato in your
pocket while working in your tomato
garden.

Sure Cure for Unsightly Warts?
Yes!

And this one purportedly does the
job!

Simply rub
over the warts with a
clean wash cloth.

Then bury the
wash cloth in a
tomato patch where
no one can find it.

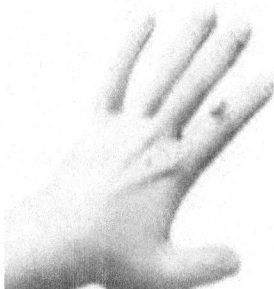

Presto!

Your warts will eventually disappear.

See a Snake in Your Tomato Patch?
Not a problem!

Get a few white geraniums.

Plant these flowers in a few places
around your tomato plants.

Snakes will no longer pay a visit to
your tomato garden.

Flies a Pest in Your Home?

White geraniums are also invaluable to households with a fly problem.

This was quite easily solved by placing a few of these flowers near any open windows.

Flies will not enter the premises.

Problem with Head and/or Body Lice?

Many families have had problems with their children coming home from school with head and/or body lice.

Solving this problem is quite easy.

Have your children eat pumpkin seeds daily as a healthy snack.

You'll get rid of such lice and never be bothered by them again.

Protect Tomato Plants From Frost

Hang some ordinary string or a stretch of yarn along each row of tomato plants.

This simple act will save the tomato plants from being harmed by frost.

Any frost will gather on the string or yarn rather than on the tomato plants.

4

Household
Hints
Using
Tomatoes

Cleaning Copper Pots and Pans
Take an old rag and lightly rub tomato sauce over the copper in a swirling motion.

The salt in and acidity of the tomato sauce will remove copper oxides and leave behind the bright and beautiful copper metal.

Getting Rid of Horrid Skunk Smell
Bathing with fresh tomato juice is one of the best known methods of removing the horrendous odor of a skunk's spray.

This can be especially important when your cat or dog happens to get sprayed by a skunk.

Removing Chlorine From Your Hair
Chlorine in a swimming pool often accidently bleaches blonde hair an unsightly green.

Thoroughly washing your hair with tomato paste will help to restore the natural blonde color!

Ripening Green Tomatoes

Put green tomatoes in a brown paper shopping bag with some apples

Apples give off ethylene gasses.

This speeds up the natural ripening process of green tomatoes.

Another Method of Ripening Tomatoes

Put the green tomatoes next to a bunch of bananas.

Bananas also give off ethylene gasses.

This gas helps tomatoes to ripen more quickly.

Wake Up With a Hangover
After a Night On The Town?

Here's a simple remedy!

1 ounce glass of tomato juice

1 shot of vodka
pinch of salt
pinch of pepper
3 drops tobasco sauce

3 drops Worcestershire sauce

Blend the above ingredients thoroughly.

Quickly down the entire sauce drink.

This is a reliable time-tested cure for a hangover.

PART 111

APHROSDIASIC
QUALITIES
OF
TOMATOES!

5

Tomatoes

An

Aphrodisiac?

Tomatoes a aphrodisiac?

Yes!

Colonists commonly called the tomato a *"love apple."*

Why?

Because many people considered them to be an aphrodisiac!

What did the following men have in common?

John Witherspoon from New Jersey
Benjamin Rush from Pennsylvania
Roger Sherman from Connecticut
William Ellery from Rhode Island
Carter Braxton from Virginia
John Livingston from New Jersey
Paul Revere

They were all well known patriots in the Colonies

The first six of these men signed the Declaration *of Independence*!

The seventh man, Paul Revere, will never be forgotten because of his heroic ride throughout the night blackened countryside to warn John Hancock and Samuel Adams as well as to arouse sleeping militiamen by yelling, *"The British are coming! The British are coming!"*

So!

What else did these men have in common?

They all fathered numerous children!

John Witherspoon of New Jersey fathered 10 children with his first wife.

She died during childbirth.

And then 68 year of age John married a 24-year old widow.

She bore him two more children to bring his total to 12 offspring!

Benjamin Rush of Pennsylvania was another productive husband.

He and his wife, Julie, produced 13 children.

William Livingston also did quite well in this department.

He and his beautiful wife, Susanna, also brought forth 13 children!

Roger Sherman of Connecticut was the father of 15 children!

William Ellery of Rhode Island was equally as prolific!

He also fathered 15 children!

Paul Revere was the father of 16 children!

Carter Braxton tops them all when it came to having a large family!

He is credited with 18 children!

And lastly, can it be assumed that each of these men consumed large quantities of tomatoes?

It is fun to consider that tomatoes increased their romantic inclinations and activities?

This was no doubt a major factor in the change of thinking regarding the tomato.

Once avoided as poisonous, the tomato later became best known as the so called *"love apple."*

And it became an accepted and highly sought after powerful and reliable *aphrodisiac!*

6

Fried Green Tomato Family Recipes of Men Who May Have Known!

The following recipes are as tasty today prepared in our homes today as they were through the years.

We wonder if the simple tomato enjoyed by notables from the American Colonies through current days contributed to larger family size.

Read, try and enjoy.

Fried Green Tomatoes
John Witherspoon
May Have Enjoyed

1 large egg, lightly beaten
1/2 cup buttermilk
1/2 cup cornmeal
1/2 tsp salt
1/2 tsp pepper
1/2 cup flour
3 large green tomatoes,
      1/3" thick slices
bacon grease as needed

Blend lightly beaten egg and buttermilk in a small wooden bowl.

Drop tomato slices in this mixture.

Combine cornmeal , salt, pepper and flour in another similar wooden bowl.

Lastly lay tomato slices in the cornmeal blend and press lightly to help it stick.

Pour ½" of melted bacon grease in a large cast-iron skillet and heat.

When hot drop in the coated tomato slices.

Fry for about 2 minutes or until lightly browned.

Flip slices over and also fry them the same way.

Drain on paper towel lined plate.

Sprinkle cooked slices with salt and pepper while hot and then serve immediately.

Dr. Benjamin Rush Might Have Been Served These Fried Green Tomatoes

1/2 cup flour
3 eggs, beaten
1/2 cup white cornmeal
3 large green tomatoes
        ½" thick slices
1 cup rendered lard
salt as needed
pepper as needed

Place flour, eggs, and cornmeal in 3 separate wooden mixing bowls.

Coat the tomatoes by dipping slices in the flour.

Next dip them in the eggs.

Let any excess egg drip off.

Lastly lay slices in the cornmeal and press gently.

Heat bacon grease in a large cast iron skillet.

When hot, drop in tomato slices.

Fry until lightly browned on both sides.

Drain cooked tomato slices on a paper towel lined plate.

Season with salt and pepper to taste before serving.

Serve immediately while still hot.

Roger Sherman Could Have Eaten These Crunchy Fried Green Tomatoes

1/2 cup cornmeal
1 tsp salt
1/2 tsp cayenne pepper
1/8 tsp sugar
4 large green tomatoes
  ½" slices
2 large eggs.
Bacon grease as required
Salt as needed
Pepper as needed

Combine all dry ingredients in wooden mixing bowl.

Drop thick tomato slices into cornmeal blend.

Cover nicely and lightly press onto surfaces.

Break eggs into another wooden bowl.

Dip coated tomato slices into eggs.

Let excess egg drip back into bowl

Lay each slice of tomato on wax paper-lined baking sheet.

Pour melted bacon grease ½" deep into a cast-iron skillet and heat to 360°.

Fry tomato slices on each side until golden brown.

This usually takes only 3 to 4 minutes.

Drain cooked tomato slices on a paper towel lined plate.

Sprinkle with salt and pepper to taste before serving.

Serve immediately while still hot.

William Ellery May Have Liked Rémoulade On His Fried Green Tomatoes

4 large green tomatoes
¼ inch thick slices

2 tsp salt
1 tsp pepper
1 1/2 cups buttermilk
1 cup white cornmeal
1 tbls Creole seasoning
2 cups flour
rendered lard
rémoulade sauce
bread-and-butter pickle slices
Preheat oven to 200°.
Slice the tomatoes to proper thickness.
Sprinkle both sides of tomatoes evenly with salt and pepper.
Pour buttermilk into a small shallow wooden mixing bowl.
Blend cornmeal, Creole seasoning and 1 cup flour in another small shallow wooden mixing bowl .
Dredge tomatoes in remaining 1 cup flour.
Dip tomatoes in buttermilk, and dredge in cornmeal mixture.
Put lard in a large cast-iron skillet.;
Heat skillet to 350°.and melt lard.
At least 1" of melted lard is required.
Fry tomatoes2 to 3 minutes on each side or until a lightly browned.

Drain cooked tomato slices on a paper towel lined plate.

Sprinkle with salt and pepper to taste.

Baste lightly with Rémoulade sauce.

Transfer to a wire rack.

Keep warm in a 200° oven until ready to serve.

Garnish with sweet pickle slices just before serving.

. Carter Braxton Certainly Would Have Enjoyed Eating These Fried Green Tomatoes

4 large green tomatoes
1/3 inch slices
1 1/2 cups buttermilk
1 tbls salt
1 tsp pepper
1 cup flour
1 cup yellow cornmeal
3 cups melted bacon grease

Cut tomatoes into ½ inch thick slices.

Put tomato slices in a small wooden mixing bowl.

Pour buttermilk over tomatoes.

Take out slices and sprinkle with salt and pepper.

Combine flour and cornmeal in a wooden mixing bowl.

Dredge thick tomato slices in this mixture.

Put bacon grease in a large cast iron skillet and melt.

Carefully lay the coated tomato slices in the hot bacon grease.

Fry tomatoes for about 3 minutes on each side. or until lightly browned.

Drain cooked tomato slices on a paper towel lined plate.

Sprinkle with salt and pepper to taste.

William Livingston Would Have Liked
These Fried Green Tomatoes

1 large egg, lightly beaten
1/2 cup buttermilk
1/2 cup flour, divided
1/2 cup cornmeal
1 tsp salt
1/2 tsp pepper
3 medium green tomatoes

Melted grease from 3 thick slices bacon

Combine lightly beaten egg and buttermilk in a wooden mixing bowl.

Set aside.

Combine 1/4 cup a flour, cornmeal, salt, and pepper in another wooden mixing bowl.

Coat tomato slices in remaining 1/4 cup flour.

Dip them in egg mixture.

Lay tomato slices in the bowl containing the cornmeal mixture.

Firmly press each tomato slice into this mixture.

Pour ½"of the melted bacon grease in a large cast-iron skillet and heat to about 375°.

Carefully put some of the coated tomato slices into the hot bacon grease and fry. .

Cook for about 2 minutes on each side or until lightly browned.

Drain cooked tomato slices on a paper towel lined plate.

Sprinkle with salt and pepper to taste.

How Fried Green Tomato Sandwiches May Have Been Prepared for Paul Revere

1 1/2 cups red cabbage, shredded
1 1/2 cups cabbage, shredded
1/3 cup red onion, sliced thin
3 tbls bacon grease
2 tbls lime or lemon juice
1/2 cup basil
Salt to suit taste
Pepper to suit taste
1/2 cup sour cream
3 tsp hot sauce
12 dinner rolls, halve and warm
12 crispy fried bacon slices
3 large green tomatoes

Blend the first 5 ingredients and 1/4 cup of the basil in a wooden mixing bowl.

Season with salt and pepper to taste.

Blend together sour cream, hot sauce and remaining 1/4 cup of basil.

Spread buns with sour cream mixture.

Cover bottom halves of buns with bacon, tomatoes, and cabbage mixture.

Cover with top halves of buns, with sour cream mixture.

Put top and bottom bun halves together and press lightly.

Serve immediately.

PART IV

A
TOUCH
OF
TOMATO
HUMOR

7

Silly

Superstitions

Regarding

Tomatoes

Never give away a cutting of one of your tomato plants or you'll have a run of bad luck!

Just leave the cutting and turn your back.

Let the person *"steal"* it!

When seeing a bee on a tomato plant you must make a point to talk to it and tell the bee the latest gossip!

To ignore the bee could bring misfortune or it may stunt the growth of your tomato plants

If a pregnant woman plants tomatoes, everything will go well with her pregnancy!

Any tomatoes sown by a pregnant woman will grow and be bountiful!

Placing a green tomato on the mantle over a fireplace when first entering a new delling is believed to ward off evil spirits!

Putting a ripe red tomato on the mantle over a fireplace upon first entering your house is said to guarantee future prosperity for the owner.

Seeing a lame horse in a tomato patch means you will have a bad crop of tomatoes that year!

A blind pig seen eating tomatoes in your garden?

Watch out!

Bad luck is foretold for the rest of your crops!

Squirrels chattering in your tomato patch means an early crop of tomatoes!

A noisy gathering of

crows in your tomato patch indicates a severe storm coming your way!

Basil must be planted at all four corners of a tomato patch at the start of the growing season.
This is said to insure a bountiful crop of tomatoes!

Take a fresh pea pod and shell it while sitting in a tomato patch.
If you count nine peas, throw one of them over you left shoulder and make a wish!

Regarding the day you find the first bloom on a tomato plant is said to be extremely important!
Monday denotes abundant good fortune.
Tuesday means your greatest attempts will turn out successful.
Wednesday denotes much happiness is foreseen.

Thursday is said to indicate small profits.

Friday indicates the coming of wealth.

Saturday denotes a good deal of misfortune.

Sunday means excellent luck for weeks to come!

It's brings bad luck to pick tomato plant blooms.

This will offend the garden fairies and make them mad.

Never milk a cow in a tomato patch and spill a drop of the milk on the ground.

The cow will dry up or so it is said!

To hear a cricket chirping in a tomato patch foretells the passing away of a family member.

The same is said to be true when hearing a whippoorwill in a tomato patch at midnight!

Sneezing while pulling weeds in a tomato patch before eating breakfast is a sign to expect visitors that day.

The same is true if you have an itchy nose while working in a tomato patch!

Plant tomato seeds before the sun comes up.
The bugs will rise from the dirt at daybreak, ignore the seeds and not eat them.

It's also said to be extremely bad luck should you pick up a strange cat in your tomato patch and carry it over your threshold and into your kitchen.

A black cat seen walking through you tomato patch while you are pulling weeds brings a curse of dire consequences!

The curse can be nullified if you turn completely around, spit twice, and take three steps toward where the cat had been seen!

Some believe that a black cat seen strolling through your tomato patch is an omen of good fortune.

But to cause the black cat's demise always brings bad luck!

A rusty horseshoe found in a tomato patch foretells bad luck unless the person picks it up, spits on it and tosses it over their left shoulder,

A rooster seen crowing in a tomato patch spells the passing of a friend or family member.

This can be avoided by butchering a hen and burying it in the middle of the tomato patch.

Never thank anyone who gives you free tomato seeds!
This is said to bring bad luck and make the seeds not grow!
Always remember to thank *only* the seeds and *not* the person who gave them to you!

If it starts to rain while you are hoeing between the rows of tomato plants then expect a bountiful harvest!

Digging up a turtle shell while hoeing between your tomato plants also portends a good harvest.

Never fertilize your tomato patch by moonlight!
It's useless and will do nothing for your tomato plants.

Rusty nails placed near the stem of your tomato plants will make them grow faster and produce more tomatoes.

Seeing a black snake in your tomato patch indicates a great harvest to come.

Hearing the coo of a turtle dove on New Year's Day indicates that your tomato plants will flourish well in the Spring or Summer.

.

Working in a tomato patch on the Sabbath will bring much misfortune.

8

Tomato Jokes

To

Tickle

Your

Taste Buds

An old man lived by himself on his farm,

He wanted to dig up his tomato garden but it was much too difficult as the ground was hard,

His only son, Johnny, used to help him with the farm chores but he was doing time in the penitentiary.

The elderly farmer sat down, wrote a letter to his son, and described his predicament,

"Dear Johnny: "I'm feeling pretty down and out because I won't be able to plant my tomato garden this year.

"I'm getting too old to be digging up a garden plot.

"If you were here, my troubles would be over.

"I know you would dig the garden for me.

"Love, Papa."

Around a week later the old man received an answer from Johnny.

"Dear Papa:

"I'd do anything for you Papa except dig up that garden.

"That's where I buried the bodies.

"Love,

"Johnny."

Early the next morning carloads of FBI agents along with the local police arrived and hastily dug up the entire garden area!

Of course they found no bodies!

The men dutifully apologized to the old man and quickly left.

The same day the old man received another letter from his incarcerated son.

"Dear Papa:

"Go ahead and plant your tomatoes now!

"That's the best I could do under the circumstances.

"Love,

"Johnny."

When does a tomato blush?
When it sees a salad dressing!

What else makes a tomato blush?
When it sees Mr. Green pea

Why is an unripe tomato round and green?

Because if it was long and skinny it would be a cucumber!

What goes up and down and is green, yellow or red?
A tomato left in an elevator!

How do you get rid of unproductive tomatoes?

Can (fire) them!

How do you tell if tomatoes have been drinking while still on the vine?

They are no more than just stewed tomatoes at this point!

How can you tell if a tomato is drinking behind your back?

They are simply tomato sauced!

What did the irritated macaroni say to the tomato?

Don't get saucy with me!

Why won't a tomato make love in a potato patch?

Because potatoes have eyes!

Why won't a tomato make love in a corn field?

Because the corn stalks have ears!

How can you repair a sliced tomato?
Glue it together with tomato paste!

Why does a tomato take out a prune?
Because it couldn't find a date!\

Why is a tomato round and red?

Because it would be a string bean if it was long and green!

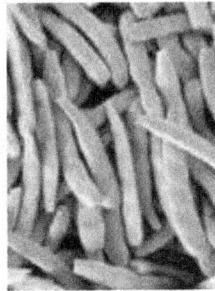

PART V

TOMATOES
&
BETTER
HEALTH?

9

Reasons

You

Should

Eat

Tomatoes?

There are quite a number of things that make the quite ordinary but highly popular tomato a nutritional powerhouse of sorts.

They are a great source of carbohydrates, fiber and iron.

Spinach also contains high amounts of iron, but it also contains high amounts of oxalic acid which prevents iron absorption.

Vitamin C can come to the rescue and help as Vitamin C aids in the absorption of iron.

Since tomatoes are such an excellent source of vitamin C, you'll get more benefits of the iron in your spinach when you eat tomatoes along with the green stuff.

Eat 1.4 cups of raw broccoli and 2.5 cups of fresh tomato (or ½ cup tomato paste or 1 cup tomato sauce) daily to get the very best nutrition benefits.

According to a study in *Cancer Research*, the tomato-broccoli combination shrank prostate tumors in laboratory animals by a whopping 52%!

The many nutrients in tomatoes put them in the *"heart-healthy"* category.

They are widely known by medical authorities to prevent many types of cancer.

Numerous other kinds of diseases are also prevented.

And tomatoes provide many additional health benefits as well.

Tomatoes have low amounts of potentially unhealthy nutrients.

Too much fat and sodium can exacerbate numerous health issues for millions.

Tomatoes are low in fat.

A tomato is more than 90% water, very low in sodium and are extremely low in calories.

Eating them often can help you feel full while not adding extra calories.

Dieters can eat a lot of tomatoes and still limit their caloric intake.

Tomatoes may have a diuretic effect that helps eliminate toxins while you're on a diet.

They certainly, therefore, fall into that special category called *"diet-friendly"*.

One cup of fresh chopped tomatoes equals 1/3 pound or one average size tomato.

Eating Tomatoes Aids Cholesterol

Believe it or not but those who consume more tomatoes are known to lower their cholesterol!

One cup of fresh tomatoes supplies the body with 9% of the mdr needed for fiber!

This has been proven beyond a shadow of a doubt to lower otherwise high cholesterol levels.

Tomatoes are also known to be a wonderful source of niacin.

Niacin is also called vitamin B3.

This vitamin has been used for innumerable years as a safe method to use for bringing down high cholesterol levels in patients.

Eating Tomatoes Aids Blood Pressure

Tomato consumption has been definitely linked to significant drops in blood pressure.

This effect was discovered during clinical research undertaken by Dr. Esther Patran, M.D. at Ben Gurion University.

Daily ingestion of a tomato extract for eight weeks showed a drop in the top blood pressure number (systolic) by 10 points!

And the bottom blood pressure number (diastolic) dropped 4 points!

Eating Tomatoes Boosts Immunity

Tomatoes are credited by medical authorities with helping people to avoid catching the flu and colds.

Drinking tomato juices assists in building defenses against viruses.

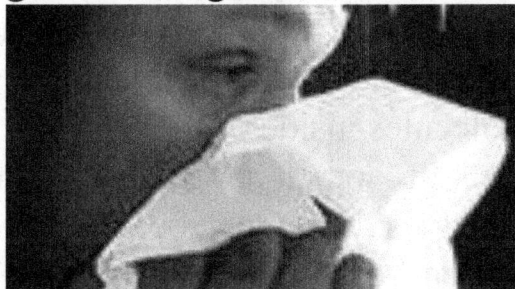

This is especially true for males.

These common illnesses are believed by most medical specialists to be rooted in what are known as carotenoid deficiencies.

Included here would be low amounts of lycopene and beta carotene in a person's system.

If you grow your own tomatoes, wait as long as you possible can before you pick them.

Vine ripened tomatoes contain nearly twice the beta-carotene and vitamin C as do their green-picked counterparts.

Eating Tomatoes Strengthens Bones

One serving of tomatoes provides 18% of the daily need for vitamin K.

Vitamin K activates what is called osteocalcin which mineralizes calcium molecules inside of the bones.

In other words, vitamin K in tomatoes helps osteocalcin do its job to harden calcium and make the bones stronger!

Eating Tomatoes Reduces Migraines?

Tomatoes are an excellent source of riboflavin.

Riboflavin helps lower the frequency of migraine attacks.

Eating Tomatoes Helps Fight Cancer

Many medical studies indicate that eating tomatoes reduces the risk of numerous kinds of cancer.

Prostate cancer is one in particular.

The Journal of the National Cancer Institute reported a study of animals that were on *"an energy-related, tomato based diet"*.

Their risk of dying from prostate cancer had dropped an astounding 32%.

A combined analysis of 21 studies published in *Cancer Epidemiology Biomarkers and Prevention* indicated that men who ate the highest amounts of raw tomatoes had an 11% reduction in risk for prostate cancer!

Those men eating the most cooked tomato products fared even better.

Their prostate cancer risk showed a 19% reduction.

Eating even small amounts of tomatoes were shown to make a difference!

Just one 6-ounce serving a day of raw tomato helped reduce the risk of prostate cancer by 3%.

Eating Tomatoes Reduces Risk of Heart Disease

A tomato has 0 grams of cholesterol and contains extremely small amounts of fat.

Tomatoes are a marvelous source of potassium.

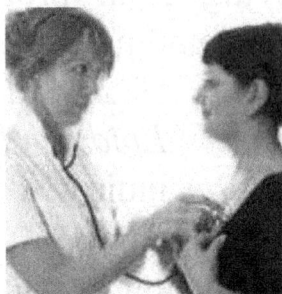

Diets rich in potassium have been shown to reduce the risk of heart disease as well as lower blood pressure.

Large amounts of Vitamin B6 and folate are found in tomatoes.

Both are needed by the body to convert a potentially dangerous chemical called homocysteine into other benign molecules.

High levels of homocysteine can damage the walls of blood vessels!

Homocysteine may be directly associated with increased risks of a stroke or heart attack!

A study of 40,000 women was undertaken at Brigham and Women's Hospital in Boston.

It was found that women who consumed 7 to 10 servings of tomatoes each week were found to have a 29% lower risk of cardiovascular disease compared to women eating less than 1.5 servings of tomato-based products weekly.

Eating Tomatoes Provides Body With a Natural Sunscreen

Researchers at the University of Dusseldorf in Germany observed subjects who ate tomato paste for a10 week period.

UV rays were absorbed 40% less than they were in the control group.

This study indicated that the lycopene in tomatoes acts as a natural sunscreen and that it provides protection against UV rays.

Eating Tomatoes Helps
Improve Eyesight

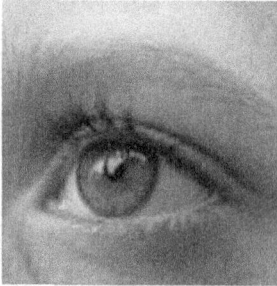

A one cup serving of fresh tomatoes provides 30% of the mdr of vitamin A.

This is essential to promoting and maintaining overall eye health.

A deficiency of vitamin A is known to contribute to the development of what is known as *"night blindness."*

One medium size tomato provides more than 1/3 of the recommended daily allowance of vitamin C and nearly 1/3 of the recommended daily allowance of vitamin A.

The tomato vitamin C content increases as the fruit ripens.

Vine ripened tomatoes contain nearly twice the vitamin C as do their green-picked counterpart.

Eating Tomatoes Helps Diabetes

Tomatoes are a good source of chromium.

Chromium has been shown to help people with diabetes.

It can help keep blood sugar levels under control.

Eating Tomatoes Protects
Against Cell Damage

Tomatoes, agree all nutrition experts, are an incredible source of the antitoxicant lycopene.

Antioxidants travel throughout the body.

They neutralize what are called *"dangerous free radicals"* that could damage cells and cell membranes.

"Free radicals" could otherwise escalate the severity of diabetes, colon cancer, asthma and atherosclerosis.

The intake of large amounts of lycopene have been proven to reduce the severity or the risk of all the illnesses.

The overproduction of free radicals within cells boosts inflammatory compounds.

These particular compounds promote virtually all chronic degenerative diseases.

Conditions such as Alzheimer's, cardiovascular disease, osteoporosis, atherosclerosis and a variety of cancers are examples.

High amounts of antioxidants lycopene and beta-carotene in tomatoes neutralize free radicals and help to reduce inflammation.

Cooking tomatoes releases lycopene for even higher effectiveness.

The antioxidant lycopene is a red pigment found in tomatoes.

Tomatoes with the most brilliant shades of red indicate that they have the highest amounts of lycopene and its fellow antioxidant, beta-carotene.

Lycopene is fat-soluble.

This simply means you'll get the maximum benefit of tomato nutrition when tomatoes are absorbed in your body with the help of fats.

Cook tomatoes with a touch of olive oil.

Or cook them with small amounts of avocado to help your body absorb lycopene more easily.

Eating Tomatoes
Counteracts Acidosis

Our bodies are specifically designed to maintain an alkaline balance with a pH of 7.365.

Yet poor exercise habits and a bad diet mean our bodies are over-acidified.

Acidosis, according to some medical authorities is a common cause of sleeplessness, fatigue, sexual dysfunction, muscle aches, headaches, hormone imbalance, arteriosclerosis, acne, eczema, depression, many degenerative conditions and calcium loss.

By including plenty of alkaline forming minerals in our diets we help our body maintain its proper balance.

These would be such things as potassium, calcium, sodium and magnesium.

Tomatoes are excellent sources of potassium, magnesium and calcium.

And they can help in preventing acidosis.

PART VI

FRIED

GREEN TOMATO

RECIPES

10

A
Variety
of
Delightful
Fried Green
Tomato Recipes

Important Pointers
On
Frying Green Tomatoes

Use solid heavy feeling green tomatoes that have been washed, dried and cut into ¼ to ½ inch thick slices.

Some cooks may prefer thinner slices but in such cases less tomato taste and more of a fry taste will be noted.

Keep the slices moist until ready to cook.

Sprinkle slices lightly with salt and minimal sugar for extra moist tomatoes that hold batter.

While assembling ingredients: Dip in flour prior to dipping in batter or eggs.

Then a second dip in cornmeal or mixture.

Use a cast iron skillet with medium to medium high heat.

Grease or oil should be hot but not smoking when adding your coated tomato slices.

Best oils have a higher smoke point such as safflower, canola, peanut or corn oil.

Refined olive oil can also be used below 350 degrees.

Turn the browned slices after a few minutes or less.

Only turn one time.

Eat immediately or hold on paper towels.

FRIED GREEN TOMATOES
WITH SALSA

2 eggs
1 1/2 cups buttermilk
1 1/2 heaping cups flour
1 tsp salt
1 tsp pepper
3 large green tomatoes cut into 1/4 inch slices
Olive oil as needed.

In a bowl, mix together the eggs and buttermilk.

Whisk in 1 tbls flour, 1/2 tsp salt and 1/2 tsp pepper.

Soak tomatoes in this for half an hour.

Whisk together remaining flour, salt and pepper.

Heat inch of olive oil to 350 degrees in cast iron skillet.

Dredge tomato slices in the seasoned flour.

Shake off excess flour.

Drop slices in hot oil and fry until crisp and nicely browned on both sides.

Drain on paper towel and salt to taste..

Serve while warm with your favorite salsa.

GREEN TOMATOES FRIED
IN BACON FAT

2 green tomatoes cut into 1/2 inch thick slices
1 tsp salt
1/2 tsp black pepper
1/2 cup white cornmeal
¼ cup flour
¼ cup olive oil
Salt and pepper tomato slices.
Combine the cornmeal and flour in large wooden mixing bowl.
Put a large cast-iron skillet over medium heat.
When hot, add enough olive oil to coat skillet.
Dust green tomato slices in cornmeal mixture just before you put them in skillet.
Don't crowd them.
Cook until well browned on both sides (3 to 4 minutes per side).
Add more olive oil if required.
Drain on paper towels and serve warm
Sprinkle with extra salt and pepper to suit taste if needed.

FRIED GREEN TOMATOES
WITH
BUTTERMILK SAUCE DIP

Oil
4 green tomatoes cut into ½" slices
salt to suit taste
pepper to suit taste
3/4 cup flour
1 tbls garlic powder
4 eggs
2 tbls milk
1 1/2 cups bread crumbs
pinch of red pepper
pinch of paprika
Heat oil to 350 degrees in cast iron skillet,
Salt and pepper both sides of tomato slices.
Blend flour and garlic powder in wooden mixing bowl.

Beat eggs and milk together in another wooden mixing bowl.

Blend bread crumbs with red pepper and paprika in third wooden mixing bowl.

Drop tomato slices in flour mixture and thoroughly coat each slice.

Then dip each slice in the milk and egg mixture.

Dip each tomato slice in egg mixture. Lastly put each slice in the spicy bread crumbs.

Now carefully place the coated slices of tomato in the cast iron skillet.

Allow to cook for about 2 to 3 minutes or until lightly browned on both sides.

Drain on paper towels and serve when coated with a special buttermilk dipping sauce.

BUTTERMILK DIPPING SAUCE

1 cup apple cider
1 tbls brown sugar
3/4 cup buttermilk
3/4 cup mayonnaise
2 tbls barbeque sauce
Juice of a lime
4 scallions, sliced thin
salt and pepper to suit taste

In a small saucepan over medium heat, combine the apple cider and brown sugar. Allow to reduce until thick and syrupy. Remove from heat and allow to cool.

In a medium bowl, add buttermilk, mayonnaise, BBQ sauce and lime juice and whisk well.

Add in the scallions and the apple cider mixture.

Cover and refrigerate until ready to serve with the fried tomato slices.

FRIED GREEN TOMATOES
WITH
HORSERADISH CREAM

4 large green tomatoes
1 cup white cornmeal
1 cup bread crumbs
2 1/2 tsp salt
2 tsp black pepper
1/2 tsp red pepper
1 cup buttermilk
1/2 cup yogurt
1 cup sour cream
1/4 cup horseradish
3 tbls lemon juice
1 quart olive oil

Carefully slice tomatoes into 3/8" thick pieces.

Lay slices on brown paper to drain.

Blend cornmeal, bread crumbs, tsp of salt, and both peppers in a wooden mixing bowl.

Combine the buttermilk and ¼ cup of the yogurt in a second wooden mixing bowl,.

Heat the olive oil in a cast iron skillet to 365 degrees F.

Dip the sliced tomatoes in buttermilk mixture.

Shake off excess.

Press tomato slices into dry mixture.

Repeat until both sides are nicely coated.

Carefully lower battered tomato slices into the hot oil.

Cook for 2 to 3 minutes until lightly browned on both sides.

Drain each browned tomato slice on wire rack or on paper towels.

Sprinkle lightly with salt while hot.

Lay tomato slices neatly on a platter.

Serve immediately with horseradish cream as made below.

HORSERADISH CREAM

Combine sour cream, remaining ¼ cup yogurt, horseradish, lemon juice and 1/2 tsp salt in small wooden mixing bowl.

Blend thoroughly.

Cover and put in ice box until ready to serve.

DEEP FRIED GREEN TOMATOES

6 cups bacon grease
1 cup flour
2 cups milk
salt
black pepper
pinch paprika
pinch red pepper
2 medium green tomatoes
2 cups bread crumbs

Heat bacon grease in large cast iron skillet

Thoroughly blend the flour and milk in a wooden mixing bowl,

Stir in the salt, black pepper, paprika and red pepper.

Cut tomatoes into 1/2-inch slices.

Dip slices into the batter.

Make certain each slice is nicely coated.

Cover both sides with bread crumbs.

Carefully drop each slice of tomato into the hot bacon grease.

Fry for 3 to 5 minutes until golden brown,

When nicely browned lay each tomato slice on paper and allow to drain.

Serve immediately while hot.

FRIED GREEN TOMATO SANDWICHES

Preparing Your Sauce

3/4 cup mayonnaise
3 tbls parsley, chopped
3 scallions, minced
2 tsp tsp hot sauce
1 1/2 tsp Worcestershire sauce
salt as needed
1 handful dill leaves
1/4 cup sugar

Preparing Your Sandwiches

6 green tomatoes
1 cup white vinegar
salt as needed
3 tbls pickling spice
2 cups flour
1/2 cup cornmeal
1 tbls chili powder
4 large eggs
Olive oil as needed for skillet
12 slices potato bread

Making Your Sauce: Blend mayonnaise, parsley, scallions, hot sauce, Worcestershire sauce and salt to taste in wooden mixing bowl. Cover and set in ice box to cool.

Slice green tomatoes ¼" or ½" thick and set aside in large wooden mixing bowl.

Blend vinegar, sugar and 1 tbls salt in a saucepan.

Tie pickling spice in a piece of cheesecloth with twine.

Drop this into the saucepan along with the dill leaves.

Let simmer while constantly stirring until sugar dissolves.

Add 2 cups cold water.

Pour this mixture over the green tomatoes.

Let sit at room temperature for 90 minutes.

Put flour, cornmeal, chili powder and 1 teaspoon salt in a shallow wooden mixing bowl and blend nicely.

Put eggs, 2 tbls water and 1 tsp salt in another shallow dish.

Pour 1" inch of peanut oil in large cast iron skillet and heat to 375 degrees F.

Pat tomato slices lightly with paper towel until dry.

Drop in the flour mixture and roll them around until nicely coated with the mixture.

Then dip the tomato slices in the egg mixture and dredge again in the flour mixture.

Carefully place tomato slices in the cast iron skillet and fry until lightly browned.

Drain on paper towels and sprinkle with salt.

Spread each slice of bread with the sauce. Layer the fried tomatoes evenly on bread slices. Cover each with the other bread slices.

SIMPLE AND QUICK
FRIED GREEN TOMATOES

Ingredients

1 cup fine cornmeal
salt and pepper to suit taste
1 cup buttermilk
1/2 cup olive or peanut oil
8 1/3" slices green tomatoes

Directions

Blend cornmeal, 1/4 tsp salt and tsp black pepper in a small wood mixing bowl.

Put buttermilk in another small wood mixing bowl.

Heat the oil in a cast iron skillet over medium-high heat.

Dip tomato slices in the buttermilk.

Coat each tomato slice with the cornmeal mixture.

Shake off the excess.

Fry until golden brown,

CREOLE SEASONED FRIED GREEN TOMATOES

Ingredients

Peanut oil to suit
2 to 3 large green tomatoes sliced 3/8" inch thick
1 tsp salt
1/2 tsp black pepper
1/2 cup white cornmeal
1/2 cup flour
2 tsp Creole seasoning

Directions

Pour 2-inches of the peanut oil in a cast iron skillet.

Heat to 325 degrees F.

Sprinkle both sides of tomatoes with salt and pepper.

Blend cornmeal, flour and seasoning in a wooden mixing bowl.

Dredge tomatoes in cornmeal mixture.

Fry until golden brown on both sides.

Take tomato slices from skillet and lay on paper towels to drain.

Eat while hot.

GARLIC AND RED PEPPER FRIED GREEN TOMATOES

1 cup white cornmeal
1 cup flour
1 tbls garlic powder
Pinch red pepper
1 1/2 cups buttermilk
Salt and pepper to suit
4 large green tomatoes, ½" thick slices
1/2 cup olive oil
1 tbls butter
Lemon wedges

Combine first 4 ingredients in wooden mixing bowl and blend well.

Pour buttermilk into a separate wood mixing bowl.

Add salt and pepper to taste.

Dip tomato slices in buttermilk mixture.

Drop each slice in the cornmeal blend.

Cover thoroughly.

Coat cast iron skillet with olive oil.

Place over medium heat.

When hot fry each tomato slice until golden brown and crispy on both sides.

Carefully remove each slice.

Drain on paper towels.

Serve with hot pepper sauce and lemon wedges.

COUNTRY STYLE
FRIED GREEN TOMATOES

2 large green tomatoes
salt to suit taste
pepper to suit taste
1/2 cup flour
1/2 cup cornmeal
1 cup bacon grease

Cut each tomato in ¼" thick slices.

Season to taste with salt and pepper.

Stir together the flour and cornmeal in a wooden mixing bowl.

Blend well.

Add bacon grease in a cast-iron skillet and heat.

Drop tomato slices in flour mixture.

Thoroughly coat both sides.

When the oil is hot, put in tomato slices and fry until golden brown and crispy on both sides.

Remove each slice and lay on paper towel.

Drain.

Serve while hot.

GREEN TOMATOES FRIED IN OLIVE OIL

2 large green tomatoes
Cut into ½" thick slices
1 tsp salt
1/2 tsp pepper
½ tsp cumin
1/2 cup cornmeal
1/4 cup flour
olive oil to suit

Sprinkle green tomatoes with the salt and pepper.

Combine the cornmeal and flour in a wooden mixing bowl.

Heat cast-iron skillet.

When hot, coat with 1/3 cup olive oil.

Lay the thick tomato slices in the cornmeal mixture and liberally coat both sides.

Put them in the skillet and cook.

Cook until well browned on both sides..

Drain each tomato slice on paper towels.

Serve while hot.

` Sprinkle with extra salt and pepper to taste.

MEET

THE AUTHOR

Robert W. Pelton has been writing for more than 45 years. And has published more than 100 books.

He proudly claims a heritage going all the way back to well before the War for American Independence.

One ancestor, John Rogers came to America on the Mayflower and was one of 41 signers of the Mayflower Compact.

John Smith was a founder of Jamestown.

Peleg Pelton served as a fifer in the Continental Army at age 17 during the Battle of Saratoga (1777) and again in Yorktown (1781).

Captain Peter Hager was Commander of the Old Stone Fort in Schoharie, New York, in 1780.

Mr. Pelton is an active member of Sons of the Revolution (SOR) whose members have descendants were in General Washington's Continental Army.

Gift copies of this book can be ordered at
www.robertwpelton.com

or

www.amazon.com

or

www.createspace.com/5180839

Orders for Resale
40% Off Retail Price

Send Purchase Order to

christianamerica2@yahoo.com

CPSIA information can be obtained
at www.ICGtesting.com
Printed in the USA
BVOW03s1910020717

488343BV00001B/13/P